WITHDRAWN

To my dear friend, Suzanne, who has kept me safe
ever so patiently, tirelessly, wisely, and lovingly.

—RD

For Bruce.

—ZL

Text © 2019 by March 4th, Inc.
Text by Rana DiOrio
Illustrations © 2019 by Zhen Liu
Cover and internal design © 2019 by Sourcebooks
The What Does It Mean to Be…?® series of children's picture books and ebooks is a registered trademark of March 4th, Inc.
Sourcebooks, Little Pickle Press, and the colophon are registered trademarks of Sourcebooks, Inc.
The full color art was painted digitally in Adobe Photoshop.
Published by Little Pickle Press, an imprint of Sourcebooks Jabberwocky
P.O. Box 4410, Naperville, Illinois 60567-4410
(630) 961-3900
sourcebookskids.com
Originally published in 2011 in the United States by Little Pickle Press, LLC.
Library of Congress Cataloging-in-Publication Data is on file with the publisher.
Source of Production: PrintPlus Limited, Shenzhen, Guangdong Province, China.
Date of Production: June 2019
Run Number: 5015151
Printed and bound in China.
PP 10 9 8 7 6 5 4 3 2 1

What Does It Mean to Be Safe?

A thoughtful discussion for readers of all ages about drawing healthy boundaries and making safe choices

by Rana DiOrio

Pictures by Zhen Liu

Little Pickle Press

What does it mean to be safe?

Does it mean beating a throw to home plate?

No.

Does it mean
never taking risks?

No.

Does it mean building walls?

No!

Being safe means…

feeling secure in your environment, protected from danger,
and learning how to respond to emergencies.

...being aware of your limits
and honoring them.

…respecting the power of things
that could harm you.

…drawing healthy boundaries with people you know.

…understanding that *yes* means yes,
and that silence is *not* yes.

...not giving in to peer pressure, and not accepting bullying.

…knowing that your problems should not be secrets.

…being able to tell someone what you think or how you feel without being afraid they will get angry or hurt you.

…having people in your life—parents, grandparents, friends, teachers— who care deeply about your well-being.

...not revealing information about yourself to strangers.

…feeling as though everyone has access
to what they need.

…choosing your own beliefs,
whom you love,

OPEN AND
AFFIRMING

WE BELIEVE
LOVE IS LOVE

and being accepted
for being you.

...checking first with your caring adult when you feel uncertain.

...believing you can ask for help,

and receive it, whenever you
really need it.

Being safe means…

listening to your inner voice and realizing you have the power to protect yourself and others.

So show your friends what it means to be safe,
and spread the word!

When we take care of ourselves, our families, and our friends, our world is a safer, more peaceful, and more joyful place.

Being safe means using our thinking skills to make smart decisions. Being safe is also a feeling we get from our surroundings. The messages throughout this book are meant to create opportunities to start meaningful conversations about all the different ways we can be safe or feel safe. But sometimes it helps to have a few examples. The following are some examples of how each phrase from the book might relate to your daily life. These aren't the only ways to think about feeling and being safe. Can you think of even more examples? If you have questions, be sure to ask a caring adult for more information!

Being safe means feeling secure in your environment, protected from danger, and learning how to respond to emergencies.

- Have a list of emergency contacts and numbers on the refrigerator or bulletin board.
- Have a family plan for big weather like tornadoes, earthquakes, or flooding.
- Attend an emergency response class as a family.

Being safe means being aware of your limits and honoring them.

- Go to sleep when you are really tired at a sleepover party, even when everyone else is still up and playing.
- Know when to say no to a playdate because you are not feeling well.
- Keep your training wheels on your bike until you are ready to try riding without them.

Being safe means respecting the power of things that could harm you.

- Don't accept a dare, like riding a horse when you don't know how or jumping out of a tree you climbed.
- Learn beach awareness and safety.
- Have a plan for when you're in a crowd, in case you're separated from your group.

Being safe means drawing healthy boundaries with people you know.

- It's OK not to want to talk about something.
- It's OK to want and have alone time.
- It's OK to tell even your closest friends and family that you do not want to be touched.

Being safe means understanding that yes means yes but silence is *not* yes.

- When someone asks you if it is OK to play with your toy, and you don't say anything, it is not OK for them to go ahead and play with your toy.
- It's not OK to think you know another person's answer without asking first and getting a response.
- It's OK to speak up when someone misinterprets your silence as consent.

Being safe means not giving in to peer pressure, and not accepting bullying.

- Seek the help of a trustworthy adult when you or one of your friends are being called names.
- Just say no.
- Learn tactics to disarm a bully.

Being safe means knowing your problems should not be secrets.

- If someone is hurting you with their words or force, you need to tell a trustworthy adult.
- If you are being treated unfairly by your teacher, you need to tell a trustworthy adult.
- If your mom's new boyfriend makes you feel uncomfortable, you need to tell a trustworthy adult.

Being safe means being able to tell someone what you think or how you feel without being afraid they will get angry or hurt you.

- You can tell your mom you don't like going on playdates at her best friend's house because her best friend's kid is mean to you.
- You can tell your dad you don't want to play baseball like he did.
- You can tell your friend you didn't like the joke he just made because it was offensive.

Being safe means having people in your life—parents, grandparents, friends, teachers—who care deeply about your well-being.

- Know that you can tell your dad you made someone else feel bad.
- Feel as though you can talk to someone when you are having problems with your parents.
- Seek advice from your aunt about how best to handle a tricky situation with a friend at school.

Being safe means not revealing information about yourself to strangers.

- Don't log on to games, apps, or websites without permission from a caring adult.
- Know when it's OK to tell someone your first and last name.
- Know when it's OK to tell someone where you live.

Being safe means feeling as though everyone has access to what they need.

- Know that your family will take care of you if you get sick.
- Know that if you or someone in your family has a disability, you will get the modifications you need.
- Know that when it gets cold outside, you have shelter and clothes to keep you warm.

Being safe means choosing your own beliefs and whom you love.

- Feel as though you are accepted even though you like things that are different from what your friends like.
- Celebrate any holiday that holds meaning for you even if your family does not feel the same way.
- Feel as though you can tell anyone you want that you love them.

Being safe means being accepted for being you.

- Wear the clothes you feel most comfortable in, even if they were not intended for you.
- Feel as though you can wear your hair however you like without being judged for it.
- Be friends with whomever you want without negative consequences.

Being safe means checking first with your caring adult when you feel uncertain.

- Ask your mom if it is OK to play with a new friend you met at the park.
- Ask your dad if it is OK to eat a berry you picked off a bush during a walk.
- Ask your aunt if it is OK to go swimming.

Being safe means believing you can ask for help, and receive it, whenever you really need it.

- If you have a problem to solve, you have a caring adult who will listen to you and help you to solve it.
- Have the confidence to ask for directions when you are lost.
- Ask for help to get down from the monkey bars.

Being safe means listening to your inner voice and realizing you have the power to protect yourself and others.

- You have the power to say no.
- You have the power to walk away.
- You have the power to say something.
- If your gut tells you it's not safe, then you should listen.
- Use your voice to be an "upstander" and speak out against bullying.
- You have the power to make someone else feel safe.

Eight everyday gestures for caring adults to connect with their child and help them feel safe and loved

1. **Play with your child** and enter their world. Find activities that you can do together, like reading stories, playing video games, playing pretend, or playing sports.

2. **Listen to your child** to help them feel seen, heard, and valued. Show them you are listening by bending down to their level, making eye contact, and putting down your phone.

3. **Be your child's cheerleader.** Tell your child what you love about them. Inspire your child to discover activities that interest them, like sports, art, music, or theater.

4. **Comfort your child** when they feel scared or overwhelmed, and practice techniques such as taking deep breaths and counting to ten. Help your child find other people and places that help them feel safe and supported.

5. **Talk to your child about their feelings.** Help them to be able to label their emotions by using a feelings chart, and model healthy ways to express feelings. Ask your child about events from their day and how they made them feel.

6. **Create calm and predictable environments.** Help your child know what to expect whenever possible by creating habits and routines. Ask yourself, what rituals would work for my family each day to make it more predictable?

7. **Set clear rules and expectations** about your child's behavior and use positive reinforcement whenever possible. Clear rules might include "no name-calling" and how often they can watch TV. Reward your child's efforts to follow family rules.

8. **Create a network of support** for you and your child, and be a support for other parents. At some point, we all need to ask for help. Whether you're helping someone else or needing it yourself, it's good to know what health, counseling, and recreation resources are part of your community.

Care for yourself too! Remember to take care of your own health and wellness so you can be there for your child. When life gets hectic, it can be hard to focus on your health. Whenever possible, take care of yourself by getting enough sleep, eating well, exercising, and going to the doctor regularly.

Focus on your healing. Hard parts of our lives can affect your health, relationships, and parenting in ways that aren't always obvious. Reach out for help—coming back from your own bad experiences will make it easier for your child to do the same.

About the Author

It has taken Rana DiOrio over four decades of healing, learning, and growth to be in a position to write *What Does It Mean to Be Safe?* Now as a mother of three children, she wants to show readers how they can protect themselves and others and to encourage caring adults to be ever mindful of their children's safety.

Rana has written her way through life—as a student, an attorney, an investment banker, an investor, an author, and an entrepreneur. She lives in San Francisco, CA, with her three children who inspire her every day. Follow Rana on Twitter @ranadiorio and on Instagram @ranedear.

About the Illustrator

As a kid growing up in China, Zhen enjoyed telling stories to her childhood friends more than anything. Today, she's still passionate about storytelling, particularly through her drawings. Aside from illustration, she loves nature and animals. She lives in the San Francisco Bay Area. Please visit her online at www.zhenLzhen.com.

Discover more
of the award-winning
What Does It Mean to Be...?® series

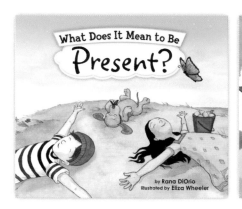

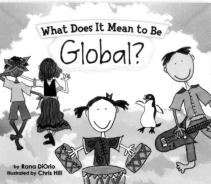

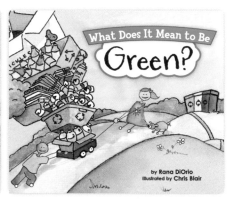

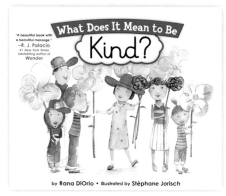

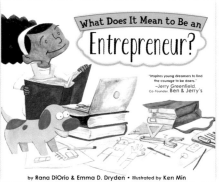

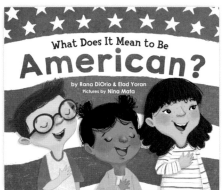